bloodlines

a play in two acts
by
Paula K. Parker

WordCrafts Theatrical Press

bloodlines
Copyright © 2013, Paula K. Parker

All Rights Reserved

CAUTION: Professionals and amateurs are hereby warned that performance of **bloodlines** is subject to payment of a royalty. It is fully protected under the copyright laws of the United States of America, and of all countries covered by the International Copyright Union. All rights, including professional, amateur, motion picture, public reading, broadcast, and any other reproduction by means known or yet to be discovered are strictly reserved.

All rights are controlled exclusively by WordCrafts Theatrical Press, 912 East Lincoln Street, Tullahoma, Tennessee 37388. No performance of this play may be given without obtaining in advance the written permission of WordCrafts Theatrical Press, and paying the requisite fee.

SPECIAL NOTE

Anyone receiving permission to produce **bloodlines** is required to give credit to the Author as the sole and exclusive Author of the Play on the title page of all programs distributed in connection with performances of the Play and in all instances in which the title of the Play appears for purposes of advertising, publicizing or otherwise exploiting the Play. The name of the Author must appear on a separate line, in which no other name appears, immediately beneath the title and in size of type equal to 50% of the size of the largest, most prominent letter used for the title of the Play. No person, firm or entity may receive credit larger or more prominent than that accorded the Author.

bloodlines
Copyright © 2013
Paula K. Parker

All rights reserved. No part of this book may be reproduced, stored in a retrieval system, or transmitted in any form or by any means – electronic, mechanical, photocopy, recording, or otherwise – without the prior written permission of the publisher. The only exception is brief quotations for review purposes.

Published by WordCrafts Theatrical Press
912 E. Lincoln St.
Tullahoma, TN 37388
www.wordcrafts.net

bloodlines

a play in two acts
by
Paula K. Parker

Playwright's Notes
on staging
bloodlines

I believe it is the responsibility of the playwright to write the play, and that it is the responsibility of the director to direct the play. As such, I have refrained from inserting many stage directions into the script, and grant the director the freedom and license to direct the show as he or she sees fit.

While it is entirely possible to produce **bloodlines** with a lavish set, I've attempted to write the play so that it can be produced on a variety of stages by theatres with either large or small budgets. A number of the roles can easily be double cast. The original production by Lab Rats Experimental Theatre in Smyrna, Tennessee used nothing more than three chairs and lighting to tell the story, and the effect was stunning.

Blessings,
Paula K. Parker

Characters
In Order of Appearance

Jake - a thief
Joey - a thief, Jake's brother
The Preacher Man - a preacher
Rorke - a prison guard/police officer
Gibbons - a prison guard/police officer
Young Joey - Joey as a boy
Young Jake - Jake as a boy.
Mama - Jake and Joey's mother
Sam - Jake and Joey's father
Bess - a girl
Danielle - a girl
Jessie - a boy or girl
Sara - a young woman
Jonnie - a friend of the Preacher
Violet - a woman
Rose - a woman
Jasmine - a woman
Alex - a man
Zane - a man
Willie - a thug
Tom - a thug
Jay - a friend of the Preacher
Attorney - the prosecutor
Mother - an older woman

ACT I

SETTING: An execution chamber.

AT RISE: Lights rise slowly. Three men are strapped into chairs. Two prison guards are standing toward the back. One has his hand on a large electrical switch. The men in the chairs are about to be executed.)

JAKE
Yeah, I got a last word for you. See you in hell!

(The guard throws the switch. The three men react to the electrical charge running through their bodies. All characters freeze. After a moment of silence JOEY rises from his chair. There is a hatch-marked shadow on the floor, as if the light is shining through prison bars. JOEY walks into the light. Lights slowly fade on the other characters, and they exit.)

JOEY
I've always hated Jake. He's my brother, and I hate him. Hated him my whole live. Now he's dying. So am I, and it's all his fault. But like it or not, we're family, and in my last moments, I've realized that being part of a family is important. It's like Jake always said - it's in the blood.

I always thought it was strange that Jake cared so much about family. It certainly wasn't that he cared anything about the individual members of the family so much – even when we were kids he used to beat me mercilessly.

> (Lights up on YOUNG JOEY and YOUNG JAKE. YOUNG JOEY is taking a beating.)

YOUNG JAKE
You're worthless, Joey. You are a waste of skin. No one cares about you!

> (Lights down on YOUNG JOEY and YOUNG JAKE.)

JOEY
But, he cared very much about "the family". With Jake it was all about upholding family traditions. And it didn't matter that our family traditions were "outside the law." You see, we were crooks; had been since before my grandfather's time, and before *his* grandfather's time. And we were very good at it. We could blend in with any crowd and feel comfortable in any situation. And of course, we were well trained in the art of thievery.

> (Lights up on JAKE and the CHILDREN. JOEY crosses to join the scene. JAKE is demonstrating pick-pocket technique.)

JAKE
The idea is to get their money without them ever knowing. Watch closely. This is where working together is important. Now.

> (JAKE crosses to JOEY and stands near him. He points to two children who start playing and wrestling. They bump into JOEY, knocking him into JAKE. JAKE helps to steady JOEY, who apologizes for bumping into him. JOEY walks

off, and JAKE hold up a wallet.) See? He thought I was helping him. What he didn't know was that I was helping myself - to his money. (The children all laugh and applaud.) This is what makes our family the best. Sticking together. Working together. Knowing how to pull off the job before you go out. Be proud of the fact that you're in this family. Be proud of your bloodlines. Now because you've all worked so hard this morning, you can have the afternoon off to play.

>(CHILDREN exit. JAKE takes off his hat and tosses it onto the chair, then exits. JOEY picks up JAKE'S hat, spits on it, throws it on the floor and grinds his heel into it.)

JOEY
As much as Jake loved the family business, I hated it. Oh, it's not like I had any qualms about the ethics of it. Take for the rich; give to the... well, we gave to ourselves. Quite frankly, it was a pretty good living. I could buy pretty much anything I liked - and I liked having the best money could buy. But I hated Jake. And I hated anything Jake loved. You're probably wondering why I didn't leave, feeling the way I did. I tried when I was a kid. But Jake always found me.

>(JOEY wanders back to his chair and sits as the lights rise on YOUNG JOEY and YOUNG JAKE, fighting.)

YOUNG JAKE
You can't run away, Joey. Like it or not, and I don't, you're part of this family. You'd never survive without us. Stealing is all you're good for. Outside of this family, you're worthless. But you try to leave again, I'll kill you myself.

>(Lights fade on YOUNG JAKE and YOUNG

JOEY.)

JOEY
I always thought death would be painful. The kind of pain that strangles all other thought. At first it is. The thought of dying consumes you. Then, as your strength gives out and the pain blurs your mind, you just kind of accept the inevitable. I always heard your life flashes before your eyes. It's true. I remember...Mama. I remember Mama arguing with Papa - usually about me.

(Lights up on MAMA and SAM.)

MAMA
Leave Joey out of this. You've got Jake. He loves this life. Joey hates it. Let him go to my folks. I'm begging you, please Sam. Let one of our children have a normal life!

SAM
Send one of my boys to your holier-than-thou family? They'd ruin him; teach him about God and all the 'thou shalt nots.' Forget it. They probably wouldn't take him, anyway. They haven't spoken to us in years.

MAMA
Can you blame them? You lied to them, and to me, about what you really do for a living. Oh, you were good. Your act was so polished, they thought you were someone they would be proud to have as a son-in-law. But you slipped up, didn't you, Sam? They found out what a con-man you really are. The only reason they haven't turned you in is to protect me and the boys.

SAM
They would never have known, if you had kept your big mouth shut.

(SAM backhands MAMA, then stomps out, leaving her weeping on the floor.)

JOEY
These fights always ended the same; Mama weeping and nursing a black eye.

(YOUNG JOEY enters and crosses to MAMA. She tries to hide her eye.)

YOUNG JOEY
Mama? What's the matter? Mama, why are you crying?

MAMA
It's nothing, Joey. I'll be alright.

YOUNG JOEY
Mama, your eye! What happened? I know what happened.

MAMA
It was an accident. I ran into… something.

YOUNG JOEY
Yeah. You ran into Papa's fist. Leave him, Mama. Run away. Today. Right now.

MAMA
I can't.

YOUNG JOEY
Why can't you? Why do you stay where you're unhappy? Where you get hurt?

MAMA
You wouldn't understand.

YOUNG JOEY
You don't still love Papa, do you? You can't love someone who hurts you so much.

MAMA
No...not anymore.

YOUNG JOEY
Then why, Mama? You're not happy here. So, why do you stay? Why? Why?

MAMA
(Lashing out.)
I stay because of you! Alright? I stay… because of you. No. I'm sorry. It's alright. Shhh. Don't you see? I can't leave because I won't leave you defenseless in this house.

YOUNG JOEY
You could take me with you. We can go away, somewhere safe. Somewhere where no one can find us. Not even Papa.

MAMA
How? I don't have any money. And your father has me watched. There might be a place I could go where he wouldn't find me. But it's not me he cares about. It's you. Don't you see, Joey. You have his blood running through your veins, and he won't let that go. Your part of his bloodline.

YOUNG JOEY
Why, Mama? Why does he do that?

MAMA
I don't know. I thought I understood him once. I even thought I loved him… once. And that he loved me. It wasn't until after we were married that I realized he hated my family so much that he wanted to steal what he considered their most precious

possession - me.

YOUNG JOEY
Why did he hate your family?

MAMA
I don't really know. I think it was because my father was a religious man; a godly man, really. Sam hates being told that anything he loves is wrong; and he loves stealing more than he loves life. Maybe that's why he won't let me leave - it would be like someone was stealing from him. So, I'll stay - for you.

> (She gathers YOUNG JOEY in her arms and begins to sing a *Lullaby*.)

I'll suffer pain for you
I'll suffer shame for you
I'll suffer humiliation for you
I'll never leave you
Never desert you
I'll always be here for you

First in my body
Then in my arms
Now in my heart
Forever I'll carry you.

MAMA
You know, Joey, when you were little, I'd take you to visit my parents. My father loved to spend time with you. He'd take you with him to the meeting house. Even as a little, little boy you always seemed to enjoy listening. You even talked about wanting to be a priest when you grew up.

YOUNG JOEY
I did? Really?! I don't remember.

MAMA
You were very young. All the other children your age would fall asleep during those long meetings. But you would stay wide awake, listening intently. You especially loved the hear the scriptures read.

YOUNG JOEY
You know, I do remember something... how did it go?..."he was numbered with the transgressors"...I don't remember what was next. Mama, what's a 'transgressor?'

MAMA
> (Slight laugh.)

That's what we are, Joey. That's what our whole family is. I remember my father telling me that was from the prophet Isaiah. I'm surprised you remembered. That was a long time ago, and you were very young.

YOUNG JOEY
I don't want to be a transgressor. I don't, Mama.

MAMA
I don't want it either, Joey. Don't worry - something will happen. I know it will. But until that time, I'll be here. I'll take care of you.
> (She begins to hum the lullaby once more as the lights fade.)

JOEY
After that, Mama and I would find time to sneak away, to talk. We'd talk about starting over - finding a place where Papa couldn't find us, where no one knew about the family. I was going to earn an *honest* living and take care of my Mama. But, I couldn't take care of her. The fights with Papa continued. He kept beating her; and she kept getting weaker. Then one day, it

was more than she could take.

> (Lights rise on YOUNG JOEY, sitting on the floor, holding MAMA.)

YOUNG JOEY
Mama. Mama. Don't die, Mama. Please don't die. Oh God, please don't let Mama die. Don't die!

MAMA
You have to let me go, Joey. I just don't have the strength to fight any more. Don't cry, Joey. I don't feel the pain anymore. My only regret is leaving you, my sweet boy.
> (She reaches up to touch his face.)

I'll always love you.

YOUNG JOEY & JOEY
Mama!

> (Lights down on YOUNG JOEY and MAMA.)

JOEY
To say that I hated my father is an understatement. I hated him even more than I hated Jake. But he wasn't in my life for too many more years. He ended up on the business end of a knife outside of some seedy bar. I was glad when he died. I thought things might be different with him out of the picture. I was right. Things got worse.

> (Lights rise on JAKE and the CHILDREN. Joey crosses to join them. He continues to narrate through the action.)

JOEY
Jake took over as head of the family after Papa's death. He ran everything. He chose the jobs, planned them, and afterwards,

divided up the loot. I tried to help, but anytime I made a comment or suggestion, it always ended the same.

>   (JAKE backhands JOEY, knocking him to the floor.)

After a while, I just shut up. Somewhere along the line I realized that, like it or not, I was a transgressor. I was a transgressor, a crook, part of a family of crooks. I hated it. But what are you gonna do? Then something happened that changed everything. It seemed insignificant at the time. Just another job as far as I was concerned.

JAKE
I've got a new job for us. This one is as sweet as pie and could set us for life!

CHILDREN
>   (Ad lib.)

Awesome! Cool! Tell us about it!

JAKE
Seems there is a new preacher in town who is drawing some pretty big crowds.

CHILDREN
>   (Ad lib.)

A Preacher? So what? Who cares? What does that have to do with us? Who is it?

JAKE
Shut up and listen! I don't know his name, and I don't care. He goes by some high sounding Biblical name that he probably made up to impress the ignorant masses. Some people will believe anything if you wrap the Bible around it. We'll just call

him...*Preacher Man*. Yeah, and we'll call our little enterprise *Operation Preacher Man*.

Alright, here's the scoop. This Preacher Man is drawing huge crowds every time he speaks. People sit spellbound for hours just listening to him. All we have to do is find out where he is going to be preaching, slip in with the crowd and slip out with their money. Those holy rollers will be so distracted by what he's saying, they wouldn't notice if you tapped them on the shoulder and said, "Pardon me, but I'm robbing you blind!"

CHILDREN
(Ad lib.)
Alright! Sounds great.

JAKE
You kids, scram outta here. I need to talk to Joey.

(CHILDREN exit, laughing and jostling each other.)

JOEY
(To the audience.)
It sounded like a sweet deal. Maybe a little too sweet. That's why, although we were all anxious to get started, Jake was his usual, meticulous self. He wanted to be sure this preacher was all he was cracked up to be. And that the crowds were suitably distracted. He decided that the two of us would check it out.

JAKE
I talked to people around town. Sounds like everything I've been told is true. This Preacher Man draws all kinds of people - rich, poor, beautiful, ugly. We'll blend right in - I'll look rich and beautiful and you'll look poor and ugly. We'll arrive at different times so that no one will suspect we're together. Don't steal anything tonight; just watch and see what goes on.

(JAKE exits.)

JOEY
The first time we followed the crowds, we discovered the preaching was going to be outdoors. After a few casual questions, I learned these meetings were held all over the place; auditoriums, homes, streets, the Preacher Man rarely showed up at the same place twice. It was weird. It was almost like he didn't want people to know where he was. Maybe he wanted people to have to seek him out. I dunno. Later that day, I met up with Jake.

(JAKE enters.)

JAKE
This is going to be the easiest job we ever pulled. Did you see those people out there? Must have been a thousand of them, all like sheep, just waiting to be fleeced.

JOEY
Yeah, I saw them.

JAKE
And there will be plenty of time to fill our coffers. That Preacher Man went on and on and on. I swear he doesn't know when to shut up. Who'd ever think I'd be happy about a sermon lasting the better part of the morning?

JOEY
Yeah, really.

JAKE
You know what was weird though? It's like it didn't seem to matter to the crowd how long he preached. Did you notice? They lapped it up like it was mother's milk.

JOEY
(Distracted.)
Yeah, I noticed.

JAKE
Did you notice, Joey?

JOEY
Huh?

JAKE
Did you notice anything, Joey?
(JAKE shoves JOEY off his chair.)
Did you notice that?

JOEY
Hey! What'd you do that for?

JAKE
Your mind is somewhere in the stratosphere. Pay attention!

JOEY
I was!

JAKE
Really? So, tell me – what did you notice today?

JOEY
Well, I heard people say this preacher is something special. Some people are saying he is more than just a preacher, that he might even be a prophet or something.

JAKE
A prophet? I don't believe in fortune-tellers. You believe in prophets, Joey? Prophets, and Big Foot, and little green men?

JOEY
I didn't say he was a prophet. I'm just telling you what I heard. That's what you want, isn't it? The details? You're always telling us, "Pay attention to the details. It's the little threads you miss that'll become the hangman's noose they put around your neck."

JAKE
You mocking me, boy?

JOEY
No...no, Jake. I'm just trying to pay attention to the details, like you said. I'm just telling you what I heard.

JAKE
That's good. Maybe you're finally starting to learn something. So Then tell me, stupid, what else did you notice.

JOEY
Like I said - most people I talked to really like him. But I also heard he makes some people uncomfortable.

JAKE
He's a preacher. They get paid to make people uncomfortable.

JOEY
No, this is different. It's like he's calling out some pretty well know folks in the religious community. He said they didn't care about God or people; that they were only interested in power and money. He said they needed to repent or else there would be hell to pay. I don't think they liked it too much.

JAKE
Truth hurts, don't it? Wish I could have been there when he said that. Boy, I bet they hate him.

JOEY
But that could mean big trouble for us. Don't you get it, Jake? They're angry because he's right about them. And they're not just gonna leave this alone.

JAKE
So, what's your point?

JOEY
What if they hire somebody to dig up some dirt on him?

JAKE
They can send the whole choir for all I care.

JOEY
Come on, Jake. They might be charlatans, but these are powerful men. They're in bed with politician all the way up to the national level. Some government leaders owe their jobs to these guys. How much do you think it would take to have our Preacher Man arrested on some trumped up charge. Then it's back to the streets to do our business.

JAKE
I see what you mean. This gold mine may not be around for long. Alright then - we'll take advantage of every chance we get. Listen, Joey, we're gonna stick so close to this guy people will think we've got religion. You should be happy. Isn't that what Mama always wanted?

(Lights fade on JAKE.)

JOEY
From that day, we focused all of our attention on Operation Preacher Man. Some days we'd take the children, other times it was just Jake and me. At first, I was too nervous to really listen to what the Preacher Man was saying. But after a while I calmed

down and started listening. So did Jake.

> (Lights up. JAKE and JOEY are inspecting the day's take.)

JAKE
Boy, what a haul today.

JOEY
Yeah.

JAKE
Seems like the harder this guy preaches, the more money we make.
> (Mock prayer)

Oh Lord, I beseech thee! Let the whole country get this kind of religion. We'd be rich!

JOEY
Yeah. Say, Jake, what do you think he meant today?

JAKE
Huh?

JOEY
The Preacher. What do you think he meant? You know, when he said, "if any man takes away your coat, let him have your cloak too." What do you think he meant by that?

JAKE
How should I know, but I wish everyone would take that to heart. It'd make our job that much easier.

JOEY
Then he said, "if any would compel you to go a mile, go with him two." And something about loving your enemies, and

praying for those who use you. Why would anyone pray for their enemies?

JAKE
I pray for my enemies all the time.

JOEY
You do?

JAKE
Yeah. I pray they'll all die!

JOEY
I don't think that is what he meant.

JAKE
Who cares what he meant? You listen up, Joey, and you listen good - you start paying attention to what the Preacher Man is saying and stop paying attention to the job, and you are gonna get caught. I swear if you get yourself caught, I won't lift a finger to help you. You understand me? If you're stupid enough to get caught, you can hang for all I care.

(JAKE exits.)

JOEY
You can hang, too, for all I care. The feeling's mutual, Jake. I hope you do get caught. I hope they leave you to rot in the hangman's noose so the birds can pick your ugly bones clean. Love your enemies, Preacher Man? You never met Jake. No one could love him. Not even God.

(The CHILDREN enter and begin playing a game on the floor. JOEY joins in.)

JOEY
We continued to follow the preacher, and it was a gravy train. Steal to our hearts' content, then come home and relax. It was business as usual, and business was good. But, before long, Jake started to change.

>(JAKE enters and scatters the game with his foot.)

JAKE
What do you think you are doing?

JOEY
We're playing a game.

JAKE
Well, stop it. There's work to be done.

JOEY
The work *is* done. The kids worked really hard this morning and I thought they deserved a reward.

JAKE
You thought? Since when do you think? I do the thinking for this family. I decide when and if someone gets a reward.
>(To CHILDREN.)

Now get out of here and find something productive to do.

>(CHILDREN exit)

JOEY
What's wrong with you, Jake? You're not acting like yourself. We always let the children play after their work was done. You said it showed them that hard work has it's rewards. Now you never let them have any fun. It's like you don't care about them anymore. Like you don't trust them anymore. Like they're not

part of the family.

JAKE
Maybe I don't trust them anymore. Maybe I don't trust *you* anymore.

JOEY
Me? What did I do?

JAKE
Don't think I haven't been watching you. You're losing your edge. Ever since we've started following this Preacher Man, you've gotten soft. You were always a slacker, never pulling your own weight. But now you're helping the kids with their chores and playing games with them? Why, I even heard you telling them a *bedtime story* last night.

JOEY
You're going all postal on me because I care about the kids? Are you saying that you don't want me to show a little kindness, a little love?

JAKE
That's exactly what I'm saying.

JOEY
You gotta be kidding. Everybody needs love, Jake. Even...even you.

JAKE
Let's get one thing straight, little brother - I don't need love. And neither do they. Love makes you soft, and when you're soft, you make mistakes. You're getting soft, Joey. You're getting weak and your starting to make mistakes. And it all started when you started listening to that Preacher Man.

JOEY
You're listening to him too, Jake. And since you started listening to him, you've grown harder. Why, Jake? What are you afraid of?

JAKE
I ain't afraid of nuthin'.

JOEY
Oh, really? I've watched you when we're out on a job, too. You don't think I pay attention, but I saw you listening to him. What's the matter, Jake? Is he getting to you? Is he making you question everything you've ever believed in all your life?

That's what he's doing to me. I've always hated this life, I just never knew why. Now I do. It's because stealing is wrong. Maybe that's what's happening to you too, Jake. Maybe you're finally realizing that your whole life is wrong; that you're wrong.

(JAKE hits JOEY and knocks him down.)

JAKE
Shut up! Shut up! If you ever say that again, I'll kill you! You understand me, boy? I swear I'll kill you! I'm not weak, and I'm not wrong, and I don't care what you or your Preacher Man thinks!

Now you listen to me, Joey. We're thieves. We've been thieves for generations. And we're gonna go on being thieves. You keep listening to this Preacher Man and you are gonna get yourself caught. I will leave you to hang, Joey, and I'll laugh as they jerk the last breath of life out of you and send you straight to hell!

(Lights fade. JAKE exits.)

JOEY
Jake was right. Listening to this Preacher Man was making me soft. I was beginning to pay more attention to him than watching what I was doing. But his words, they were so powerful. I had heard the scriptures read when I was very young. And later when Mama and I would hide out, she'd try to remember some of the scriptures her father had told her when she was little. It was our way of rebelling against Papa. But, I never heard words like this man spoke. It was like they were burning their way into my soul.

(Lights up on JAKE sorting through some loot.)

JOEY
That was some crazy stuff the Preacher Man was saying today, huh, Jake?

JAKE
What?

JOEY
The Preacher Man. I said he was talkin' crazy today. Did you hear what he said?

JAKE
Yeah, some.

JOEY
What do you think he meant by all that death and life stuff?

JAKE
What death and life stuff? What are you talking about? Did he see us? Did anybody see us taking something?

JOEY
Nobody saw us. Relax, that's not what I meant.

JAKE
Don't scare me like that. So, what did he say?

JOEY
He was talking about being dead and then being alive again. He said something about passing from death into life. He said every one who sees the Son and believes on him, has everlasting life. What do you think he meant by that, Jake? Who is this Son he keeps talking about? Sounds like he was saying we could live forever.

JAKE
That's just crazy talk. When you die, you're dead. Period. Get it through your head, Joey, there ain't no sweet by-and-by, and there ain't no such thing as miracles.

JOEY
I don't know, Jake. I heard some people in the crowd talk about miracles and…

JAKE

(JAKE feigns a televangelist posture.)
Yeah, yeah, I know – 'Oh, come out, you foul spirit! Heal! Say Ba-by!' Can you not shut up about it! I'm tired of hearing what this Preacher Man says or what this Preacher Man does, or what people think or say about him. I don't care!

JOEY
Don't you want to know how to live forever?

JAKE
Oh, fer the love of… Listen! There is no living forever! This life is all there is! That's it. Nobody is going to give you nothing, so you better get all you can and can all you get, and if you're lucky you might have a little time to sit on your can.

(Lights fade on JAKE.)

JOEY
Inside, I knew Jake was wrong. This isn't all there is. It can't be. Don't ask me how I knew. I just knew. Maybe I wanted to believe because I wanted to think I had another chance for happiness somewhere in the future. I thought, if there was, maybe I'd see Mama again. I don't know. All I know is that I began thinking a lot about what the Preacher Man said.

The problem was that he also talked about repenting. Now there's a concept. You couldn't just *say* you were sorry, you had to actually *be* sorry. That was going to be tough. I mean, I felt bad about stealing, ya know? I had for some time. But no one in my family had ever quit stealing. It's the family business. Yeah, right. Try explaining that to God.

(JOEY Awkwardly kneels.)

JOEY
God? I've been hearing a lot about you lately. About how much you love us and want us to live a good life. Okay, God, here's the deal. I know that stealing is wrong. I'm sorry every time I steal something. But, I don't know how to stop. And Jake. He'd kill me if I tried to leave the family. The only way I can quit being a thief is if Jake dies. Or I do.

So, the ball's in your court God. What do I do? Live as a thief, or die as a… as a what?

(Fade to black.)

ACT II

SETTING: JAKE'S apartment.

AT RISE: Lights rise on Jake and Joey discussing their next move. BESS sneaks up behind JAKE and attempts to pick his pocket. JAKE feels it, pulls a knife, turns and grabs the child.

JAKE
What d'ya think you're doing?

JOEY
Whoa, Jake! What are you doing? Let her go!

JAKE
Shut up! This little thief was trying to pick my pockets. Nobody steals from me. Nobody!

BESS
Jake...please....I was just practicing, like you told us. It was just a game. I made a bet with the others. I bet them I could pick your pocket and you wouldn't notice. Please Jake. It was just a game. I wasn't really going to steal from you. Honest.

JAKE
A game? You think this is a game? It was a stupid game. It could get you killed. Go on. Get outta here.

(BESS exits.)

JOEY
Jake, what's gotten into you? You could have hurt her.

JAKE
Yeah, so?

JOEY
Whaddya mean, 'so'?! And what's up with the switchblade, Jake? Papa never carried a knife. Never allowed us to carry *any* weapons. He always said it was bad for business. Said it caused too many questions. Might draw attention from the pigs. Might create more trouble than we wanted.

JAKE
Yeah, well, Papa is dead! I lead the family now. Trouble comes whether you look for it or not Joey. And I, for one, am going to be ready for it. A man's gotta protect himself.

JOEY
Protect himself from what? A buncha little kids? What if the wrong person sees you with it? Those things are illegal, ya know. What if a *pig* sees it?

JAKE
Illegal?! That's rich! I tell you what, Joey, if a pig sees it, then that's the night I bring home a pig's liver for supper!

(JAKE exits.)

JOEY
Jake was definitely changing. We all knew it - *he* knew it. And it was all because of the Preacher. The more he preached about love, the more Jake hated. The more he preached about goodness, the more evil Jake became. Even his concern for the family was dying and all he cared about was himself. His needs. His wants.

(JOEY exits. Lights up on the children. JAKE is watching from the corner.)

DANIELLE
You look different today.

SARA
How do you mean?

JESSIE
Well, you look cleaner, for one thing.

SARA
Shut up!

JESSIE
No, she's right. You do look different. You combed your hair.

DANIELLE
And put on your best things. You even *smell* better. I bet I know what's going on. Sara's got a boyfriend.

SARA
Shut up! I do not.

JESSIE & DANIELLE
Sara's got a boyfriend! Sara's got a boyfriend!

BESS
Leave her alone. I think she looks pretty.

SARA
Thank you, Bess. You're sweet...unlike *some people* I know.

(JESSIE and DANIELLE continue to their taunting. BESS starts to fight them. JAKE crosses and puts a stops to ruckus.)

JAKE
What's going on?

CHILDREN
(Ad Lib.)
Nothing Jake. We were just playing.

BESS
(Still fuming.)
They said she looks different! They said she smells good!

JAKE
Get outta here.
(The children start to leave. JAKE grabs SARA'S arm.)
Not you.
(The other children exit. JAKE circles her, looking her over.)
They're right. You do look different.

SARA
What d'ya mean? It's just me. Sara. Same ol' girl.

JAKE
No, you're not the same ol' girl. You're growing up, Sara. You're taller. Slimmer.
(JAKE stops very close behind her. He lifts her hair to his nose and inhales. Things are starting to get creepy.)
Prettier. You know, maybe we should expand the family business.

SARA
I don't understand.

JAKE
Well, thievery has always been a profitable enterprise, but maybe it's time we got into the adult entertainment business...starting with you. In fact, I could begin your training right now.

> (JOEY enters and sees what is happening. He is incensed. He jerks JAKE away and hits him, knocking him to the floor.)

JOEY
What d'ya think you're doing, Jake?

JAKE
Get outta here, Joey. This is between her and me.

JOEY
No, Jake. This is between you and me. She's family. You can't do that to her.

JAKE
I can do whatever I want with her. The way I see it, she'll be more valuable to the family after I'm finished with her.

JOEY
> (To Sara)

Go on. The others are worried about you. Go! Nothing's going to happen to you. I promise.

> (SARA exits as JAKE gets to his feet.)

JAKE
You shouldn't have interfered, *Little Brother*. It wasn't your business.

JOEY
Jake, you always said we were supposed to protect the family. If anyone else had tried that with her, they'd already be dead.

JAKE
Yeah, well, it wasn't *anyone else*. It was me. And I wouldn't have hurt her. Not any more than necessary.

JOEY
She's a child! She's family! Jake, this is wrong!

JAKE
She's a *child!* She's *family!* It's *wrong!* You sound just like Mama!

JOEY
Don't you talk about Mama!

JAKE
Mama was such a *whiner.* 'Don't do this.' 'Don't do that.' 'That's not right.' 'Why can't you be a good little boy, like Joey?'

JOEY
Shut up! Just, shut up!

JAKE
I got tired of hearing her whine. I was glad when she died.

JOEY
I said shut up!

(JOEY lunges for JAKE. This time JAKE is ready for him and knocks him down. He pulls his knife and holds it to JOEY'S neck.)

JAKE
Something else you wanted to say to me, boy?

JOEY
Jake, I...I'm sorry.

JAKE
Damn right you're sorry. If you weren't my little brother you'd be dead.
>(JAKE pulls the knife away and starts to walk away.)

JOEY
Jake....

JAKE
Get away from me, Joey. Get out and don't come back. I said get outta here... before I change my mind and kill you anyway!

JOEY
But Jake, where would I go. We're family, remember? We have the same bloodlines. We need each other.

JAKE
I don't need you, Joey. I don't need anyone. Now get outta here, and take those bratty kids with you. I don't ever want to see you again.

JOEY
Jake...

JAKE
Are you deaf, dumb, blind and stupid? What part of 'Get outta here,' didn't you understand?

JOEY
Goodbye, Jake.

           (JOEY exits.)

JAKE
Don't ever let me see your ugly face again! You hear me, boy? The day you see my face again is the day you *die*!

           (Lights down on JAKE. Lights up on JOEY.)

JOEY
I couldn't believe it. I was free. The thing that I had longed for all my life, the thing I had even prayed for, had finally happened. I was free of Jake. Free to make a new life for myself.

           (CHILDREN enter. JOEY gives them some money.)

JOEY
Here. This is all I could find. I wish it were more.

BESS
I don't want to take your money, Joey.

JOEY
Well, technically it's not mine. I know where Jake stashes his emergency funds, and this seems to qualify as an emergency to me.

SARA
You should keep some of this, Joey.

DANIELLE
Yeah, Joey, you'll need it.

JOEY
I'll get by just fine. Don't worry about me. Besides, it's a long way to my grandparents' house. You'll need all of this for the trip.

JESSIE
But what about you, Joey? Aren't you coming with us?

JOEY
Not now. Maybe later. Now, hurry, before Jake comes back and finds his money missing.

> (The children each hug JOEY and ad lib goodbyes. SARA is the last to leave.)

SARA
Joey, thanks. For this. For everything. For this morning.

JOEY
Are you okay?

SARA
Yeah. I was a little scared. Jake has never acted that way before.

JOEY
I know. I'm sorry.

SARA
Hey, it's not your fault. It's just that Jake is, well, Jake is Jake. He's always been hard. It's not like you could ever get close to him. But in his own way I think he really cared about us. Cared about the family. But lately....he's changed somehow. I don't understand.

JOEY
I know.

SARA
You've changed too, Joey.

JOEY
What d'ya mean?

SARA
You're nicer. Easier to be around. Used to, you kept to yourself all the time. And honestly, you were as bad a Jake about only caring about yourself. Now here you are giving us all your money, arranging for us to go to your grandparents home to live.

JOEY
Oh...well...you see...

SARA
You don't have to say it, Joey. I understand. But what about you? What are you going to do, now?

JOEY
I don't know yet. It's funny. All my life I wanted to stop being a crook. Now I realize that I don't know how to do anything else. But you have to get going. Watch out for the children. Try to make them behave. And remember – you're family.

SARA
I will. Thanks again. Goodbye, Joey.
    (She starts to leave, then turns back.)
Joey, I....I love you.
    (SARA exits.)

JOEY
I love you too.
    (JOEY watches her go, then looks up to heaven and attempts a prayer.)
Uh...God. Take care of them. Help them to forget this life. It will

be hard for them there, I know. But I've changed, so I know they can change too. And God, I don't know what to do now or even where to go. But I wanted to thank You for answering my prayers. I want to do good. I just don't know how. For me to live right would take a miracle. But, hey, after today, I gotta believe in miracles, right?

(Lights down. Lights rise on JOEY)

JOEY
That was the most wonderful day in my life. It was like I had been set free. It's funny - I had no home, no money, no family, no nothing, yet I felt rich. I felt like a kid; like I had been born again. I remember wandering up to a fig tree on the side of the road and picking one. I had never eaten anything that tasted so good. It was a perfect day. I wanted to laugh, to shout, to dance, to cry. But most of all, I wanted to find that Preacher so I could tell him what happened.

Like he would know me from Adam.

It wasn't hard to find out where he was preaching. The town was on fire about him. There was a big outdoor revival going on, and all you had was follow the crowd. Just to show you that God has a sense of humor, he preached about food that day. I only had one fig in my stomach, and there he was, talking about bread.

(All actors begin gathering, and sit on the floor as the preacher speaks.)

PREACHER MAN
The living bread came down from heaven: if any man eat of this bread, he shall live for ever. Believe me when I tell you that unless you eat the flesh of the Son of Man, and drink his blood, you have no life in you. But if you eat this bread you will live forever.

>   (PREACHER MAN exits. Crowd begins to mill around.)

JOEY
I didn't have a clue what he was talking about, yet, his words stirred something inside of me. I wanted to learn more about this bread from heaven that gives eternal life. Unfortunately, thinking about bread reminded me that my stomach was empty. I had no money, no job, and no experience other than picking pockets. Of course, I was through with a life of crime. No more stealing for me. But I sure was hungry.

>   (JOEY walks through the crowd and smiles as he holds up a wallet. He starts to walk away, then stops, turns and taps JONNIE on the shoulder.)

>   **JOEY**

Excuse me – Ma'am?

>   **JONNIE**

Yes?

>   **JOEY**

I...think this might be yours.

>   **JONNIE**

Why yes, it is. Thank you. I don't know how it fell out of my purse.

>   **JOEY**

Well, to be honest, I...

>   **JONNIE**

It doesn't matter. What does matter is that you were honest enough to return it to me.

>   (She opens the wallet and pulls out some bills.)

Here - this is for you.

JOEY
No, really, I couldn't.

JONNIE
I insist. There are plenty of others who would've thought, 'finders keepers.' I believe in rewarding honesty. Please, take it.

JOEY
Thank you.

(Everyone except JOEY exits. JOEY looks up to heaven.)

Thank you.

(Lights fade then rise. Several people are seated or standing, chatting.)

JOEY
I stopped by a little café to grab some chow. I wasn't going to spend much. I didn't know how long it would take me to find work, and I wanted to make what little I had last as long as possible. While I was paying for my meal I overheard people talking. Apparently the Preacher Man had ticked off some very important people, and folks in town were beginning to take sides.

VIOLET
And you know who he's got singing in the choir?
(Whispers in ROSE'S ear.)

ROSE
You're kidding? Doesn't he know what kind of woman she is? She just got out of jail for drugs and prostitution. It was all over the news.

VIOLET
You know I'm not one to listen to rumors, but they say he's 'keeping' her, if you know what I mean.

ROSE
No! He couldn't be.

VIOLET
It doesn't surprise me. He wouldn't be the first evangelist with a woman on the side. I'm not saying that's what's happening. I'm just telling you what I heard.

JASMINE
Well, personally, I used to like him. He seemed like such a humble man. But not anymore. He's gotten way too full of himself.

ROSE
What do you mean?

VIOLET
My husband went up to him to find out who he answers to. I mean, everybody should be accountable to somebody, right?

ROSE
What did he say?

ALEX
He told me that he was accountable to no man. He said that he answered to God alone.

ZANE
I heard they are auditing his taxes. Seems he told a bunch of people that taxes were for servants.

ALEX
The feds didn't take it too kindly. They'll dig up some dirt on him. You can count on it.

VIOLET
He's not getting much sympathy with the rest of the ministers in the area either. I heard he called one of the most prominent preachers in town a snake in the grass who was only interested in fleecing the flock.

ZANE
Where does this guy get off? I mean, who does he think he is, God?

JASMINE
All I can say is, he'd better watch his back. His tongue is going to dig his grave.

> (JOEY leaves the café. Before he gets too far he encounters two old acquaintances. One bumps into him, rather hard.)

JOEY
Hey, watch where you're...

WILLIE
Well, if it ain't little Joey. Hey, look Tom, it's little Joey. Where ya' been keep yourself lately, Joey?

TOM
Yeah, Joey, we haven't seen you around much.

JOEY
I've been around.

WILLIE
We haven't been doing much business with you lately, Joey.

JOEY
Well, I....

(TOM Interrupts)

TOM
We heard you "retired" from the business, Joey.

JOEY
Retired? Why that's... Who told you that?

TOM
Jake told us that. He said you got religion. He said you didn't want to hang around with guys like us no more. We got our feelings all hurt.

JOEY
Do you know where Jake is?

WILLIE
It don't matter. Jake don't want to see you no more, Joey. Fact is, Joey, he thinks all this "righteous living" of yours might mess up your loyalties. He thinks you might turn him in. He thinks if you would turn in your own brother, you'd turn in us, too. I told him, 'Naw.' I says, 'Jake, Joey's just scamming. He's not gonna turn nobody in.' You ain't gonna turn nobody in, are you, Joey?

JOEY
No. no. I wouldn't turn anybody in. Even if I wanted to, who'd I go to? Who'd believe me?

TOM
That's the way to think, Joey. Didn't I tell you little Joey had a head on his shoulders. After all, little Joey knows, if they

arrested Jake, *or us,* ain't no telling *whose* name might come up in the conversation. Ya' know what I mean? Somebody could end up dead. Ya' know what it mean?

WILLIE
Ya know you're right. One of us goes down, we all go down. Ain't that right, Joey?

> (JOEY nods and starts to leave.)

TOM
Ya know, Joey, it's like Jake always said. You got this in your blood. The only way you'd leave this business is dead.

> (TOM and WILLIE exit.)

JOEY
I found work on a farm outside of town. It was hard work, but honest. It didn't pay much, but it included room and board. For the first time in my life I actually enjoyed the feel of dirt under my fingernails.
It had been several weeks since I had made it into town. I was looking forward to a day off when I could just wander the streets, and maybe buy something with my first legitimate paycheck.
When got to town, news about The Preacher was on everybody's tongue, and most of it had a bitter, hateful taste. It was the holiday season – a time when you expected to smell love in the air. But the atmosphere in the city was as heavy as a shroud.
I wanted to find that preacher, to tell him what his ministry had meant to me, personally. As fate would have it, that very day I ran into a couple of people who had shared the platform with him the first time I heard him preach.

> (JAY and JONNIE approach. They are deep in conversation.)

JAY
Look, all I'm saying is he needs to back off of that whole, 'if you claimed to love God and hated your brother you were a liar,' thing.

JONNIE
Why? What's your problem?

JAY
What if you have a good reason to hate your brother? When my old man died, my brother got everything. I got nothing. How's that fair? Now, I love God, but he's telling me I have to love that bloodsucking mongrel of a brother of mine?

JOEY
Excuse me. Don't you hang around with that preacher, Joshua Davidson?

JAY
Lots of people hang around with Joshua.

JOEY
No, what I mean is…

JONNIE
We know what you mean. You'll have to forgive Jay. He gets a little cantankerous at time.

JOEY
I want to see him; speak with him. Is that possible? Can you take me to meet him?

JAY
Maybe you'd like us to arrange dinner?

JOEY
Could you do that? That'd be great!

JAY
No. We can't do that. Look, friend, everyone wants to see Joshua. But he's a very busy man and we can't just...

JONNIE
Once again you will have to forgive my friend. But, unfortunately, he's right. A lot people want to see Joshua, and mostly for selfish reasons. They all want something from him – you understand. Jay here takes care of the finances for the ministry. It bothers him that Joshua is so generous. Jay feels if we don't watch out for his best interests, nobody will.

JAY
If I didn't keep a tight watch on the money, he would give away every penny we have.

JONNIE
What 'We'? It's the ministry's money, not ours. And you're right. He would, and without a single regret. So, what is it? Do you need money? I don't have much but...

JOEY
No, I don't need your money. That's not why I want to speak to the preacher. I just wanted to...

>   (A number of people wander through the scene including JAKE, who is reaching into a ROSE'S purse. JOEY sees him.)

JOEY
Look, I'm sorry. I've got to go.

>   (JAKE sees JOEY and startles. ROSE realizes

what is going on and starts a commotion starts. JAKE doesn't seem to notice. He is intent on getting to JOEY.)

JAKE
Hey! You! You stole my money! *My money*! I want it back – y' hear?!? Nobody steals from me. Give me back my money, you little thief.

ROSE
Hey! What are you doing? You thief! You're trying to steal my money! Help! Police! Someone call the police!

(JAKE tried to hold onto her purse while also trying to get to JOEY. ROSE refuses to let go, and begins fighting back. JAKE pulls out his knife to threaten her. JOEY sees it and rushes forward to try to stop him. JAKE stabs ROSE.)

JOEY
Jake! No!!

(RORKE & GIBBONS arrive and wrestle JAKE to the ground.)

JASMINE
(Pointing at JOEY)
He was in on it too. They know each other. I heard them.

JAKE
Yeah, I confess. We were working together. He's my brother; my partner in crime.

(RORKE grabs JOEY.)

JOEY
Jake, don't do this.

JAKE
I told you, Joey. I told you the next time I saw you would be the day you died. I told you. You can never get away from me. Never! It's in the blood.

>(Blackout. Lights rise slowly on a court room.)

JOEY
Jake was right. I guess that's what happens when you have bloodlines like mine. Because of my bloodlines I lost my mother, the one person I truly loved. Because of my bloodlines I lived a life I hated. And now, because of my bloodlines, I'm dying for something I didn't do.

Our trial was a sham. We didn't have a chance. Turns out that woman Jake killed was a policeman's wife. It was just my bad luck to be in the wrong place at the wrong time. The fact that I was innocent didn't get in the way of the wheels of justice. So much for the truth setting me free.

ATTORNEY
Were you a witness to the crime?

JASMINE
Yes, I was.

ATTORNEY
Would you please tell us what you saw that day?

JASMINE
Well, I was minding my own business, shopping for the holiday, when I noticed that man
>(Points at JOEY)

walking down the street opposite me.

             ATTORNEY
What was he doing?

             JASMINE
Well, he tried to look like he was shopping. But he seemed nervous. He kept looking around, like he was afraid of being seen.

             ATTORNEY
And then...?

             JASMINE
Well, I got suspicious, you know? I wondered if he was up to something. I decided to watch him. I thought it was my civic duty and all.

             ATTORNEY
Of course.

             JASMINE
Then this man
            (Points to JAKE)
comes up from the other direction. He moved real slow and stayed close to people. I saw him reach into that woman's pocketbook. Then he looked over at that man
            (Points to JOEY)
who gave him some kind of signal, because all of a sudden, he started yelling, "Thief!" and then everything went crazy. He
            (Points to JOEY)
started yelling, then he
            (Points to JAKE)
pulls a knife. Then everybody was yelling and a crowd started to gather and he
            (Points to JAKE)

lunged out and stabbed her. It was awful.

ATTORNEY
So, you believed you saw these two men working together in a pick-pocketing scheme that went bad?

JASMINE
That's what it looked like to me.

>(Lights fade on courtroom, then slowly rise on JOEY.)

JOEY
I didn't see much sense in trying to defend myself. What was the use? Jake agreed with everything the witnesses said. It was all a lie, but sometimes lies seem easier to believe than the truth.

And how could I explain why I didn't run away when I saw Jake with the knife? Funny as it sounds, for the first time in my life, I had the opportunity to help my brother; to try to keep him from doing something stupid. Sounds crazy, I know.

The pain is getting stronger now. I can't keep fighting it. It won't be long now and it'll be over. I'll be free, at last. I didn't feel that way yesterday. I was scared and mad - mad at Jake, mad at life, mad at God.

>(Lights up full to reveal a jail cell.)

JOEY
What's going on here, God? I'm innocent. The preacher said truth is stronger than lies, and I believed him - right up to the time they found me guilty and sentenced me to death. To death! Where are you?

They're going to kill me, God. I'm going to die, and what

happens then? The preacher said when you die that you don't really die – but that your soul lives on. I never got to ask him what he meant. Does that mean there really is a heaven, and that I could go where Mama is? I'd like to see Mama again.

(Lullaby music plays softly in the background. Lights rise to reveal JAKE in the next cell.)

JAKE
If it isn't my little, wimp brother, still whining for his mama.

JOEY
Shut up, Jake.

JAKE
Don't tell me to shut up. You shut up, you little wimp! If I could get my hands on you I'd…

(RORKE enters.)

RORKE
Shut up, both of you! I'm trying to get some sleep. If either of you give me any problems I'll…

JAKE
You'll what, pig? Kill me? Well, ain't I scared? Why don't you come in here and I'll show you some problems. Pig!

RORKE
You know, Jake, I watched them getting ready for your execution tomorrow. It's going to be a big event. They fixed it so lots of people can see you writhe. You know what? I'm on duty tomorrow. I'm the one who gets to flip the switch. Don't you worry none about it being over quick. I know lots of tricks to make it last a long time. Death will be slow in coming for you, Jake.

JAKE
You Pig!

JOEY
Hey! Guard?

RORKE
What do you want?

JOEY
I want to talk to a preacher.

RORKE
A preacher? What would someone like you have to say to a preacher? You want to pray and beg for forgiveness?

JOEY
I want to talk to a preacher. I want to talk to Joshua Davidson.

RORKE
(Laughs.)
Joshua Davidson, huh? Don't worry. You'll see Davidson before you die. He'll be there. I guarantee it.

(RORKE exits.)

JOEY
Jake? Hey, Jake?

JAKE
Shut up.

JOEY
Jake, are you alright? Jake?

JAKE
Like you care.

JOEY
Actually...I *do* care.

JAKE
Right. Yeah. Sure you do.

JOEY
Jake, you're my brother. We...

JAKE
Look! I don't know what scam you're running, but let's get one thing straight. I don't care about you. You don't care about me. The fact that we happen to be brothers is our parents' fault, not mine.

JOEY
You're wrong, Jake. I do care about you. Look, I know I hated you in the past. But, Jake, in less than a day we'll be dead. I don't want to die with hatred on my conscience. When I die, I want to know that, at least at the end, things were right between us. After all, like you always said, we're family. It's in the blood. Look, I don't know how to say this. Jake, I'm sorry. Could we at least - die - friends?

JAKE
Suddenly you want to be friends? You want me to love you? Look, little brother, you can talk to your preacher tomorrow about forgiveness and love, but leave me out of it. I don't need love. I got hate. Hate made me strong. Hate made me sharp. Hate kept me going. Hate's all I ever had. And tomorrow, Hate'll take me, kicking and screaming all the way down to Hell.

(Lights fade, then rise. RORKE & GIBBONS

enter.)

GIBBONS
It's time, gentlemen.

JAKE
It's about time, you pigs!

> (JAKE spits at them. RORKE punches him in the stomach.)

GIBBONS
Thanks, Jake. I've been wanting an excuse to do that.

> (GUARDS escort JAKE and JOEY to their chairs and begin strapping them in. The gallery is filled with all of the other cast members. The mood begins to gradually shift, taking on a 'twilight zone' feel.)

JOEY
Wait. You promised I could see the preacher before I died. You promised I could see Davidson.

RORKE
Never let it be said I'm not a man of my word. I'm gonna go get him for you right now.

> (RORKE exits, then returns with the Preacher, in chains. MOTHER rushes from the gallery and embraces him. JONNIE follows.)

MOTHER
Jesus, what have they done to you?!

PREACHER MAN
Mother. What are you doing here? You shouldn't be here.

MOTHER
I'll go to the governor. I'll beg for clemency. You don't have to do this. Please.

PREACHER MAN
Yes, Mother, I do. Jonnie, please, take her home. And take care of her.

JONNIE
I will.

PREACHER MAN
Please, Mother, go with Jonnie. Please. She'll look after you. We will see each other again. I promise. Now go.

(JONNIE leads MOTHER back to the gallery. RORKE pushes him toward the chair.)

PREACHER MAN
Please, sir. I'm thirsty.

(RORKE reaches into a bucket of water beside the chair and pulls out a sponge. He thrusts it into the PREACHER'S mouth.)

RORKE
Thirsty, huh? We usually squeeze the water onto the condemned man's head. Makes the electricity flow through your body more quickly. Makes the death less painful. But you can drink it instead. To bad there's not enough to anoint you with. This execution is gonna hurt.

PREACHER MAN
I forgive you. You don't know what you're doing.

RORKE
(Pulls the straps tight.)
Oh, I know what I'm doing, alright. I know exactly what I'm doing.

ATTORNEY
Ladies and gentlemen of the gallery. Before you are three condemned men. You are here to witness their execution. To my left, Jacob Ben Samuel, guilty of theft and murder. To my right, Joseph Ben Samuel, guilty of theft and murder. Between these thieves, Joshua Davidson, guilty of sedition and treason.

MOTHER
My son is innocent. He's innocent. Please.

JASMINE
Innocent? I heard him say he would tear down the temple and rebuild it in three days.

SARA
He's crazy. I heard him say he was the Son of God.

RORKE
All that talk about saving others. He can't even save Himself.

GIBBONS
If can get out of the chair alive, then we'll all believe in him.

RORKE
Hey, you want to make a little wager? I'll bet you this guy's clothes he's the first one to die.

GIBBONS
You're on!

JOEY
Davidson?

MOTHER
He was numbered with the transgressors.

JOEY
What are you doing here? You're innocent.

BESS
He bore the sins of many and made intercession for transgressors.

JONNIE
It is expedient that one should die for the people.

JOEY
I don't understand. Why won't you talk to me?

>(MAMA Begins softly singing her lullaby. MOTHER joins in.)

YOUNG JAKE
He was despised and rejected.

RORKE
A man of sorrows.

ROSE
Well acquainted with grief.

GIBBONS
We considered him stricken of God, and afflicted.

DANIELLE
As a sheep before her shearer, he opened not his mouth.

JAKE
So you're the great Joshua Davidson. Not so high and mighty now, are you?

YOUNG JOEY
He was wounded for our transgressions.

ATTORNEY
Bruised for our iniquities.

JAKE
If you're so great, why don't you spring yourself, and take us with you?

JESSIE
The chastisement of our peace was upon him.

VIOLET
And with his stripes we are healed.

JAKE
Because you can't! You're nothing but a fraud. A fake. You're a liar! A liar and a thief! You steal men's dreams and make them think they might be better than the worms they are. You make them believe there might actually be a God who loves them. Well, I don't believe. I hate you! Do you hear me Son of David? I hate you!

JOEY
Shut up! Don't you fear God even now? We're only getting what we deserve. But this man has done nothing wrong.

ATTORNEY
Jacob Ben Samuel, Joseph Ben Samuel, Joshua Davidson – you have been tried and found guilty of high crimes and misdemeanors. You have been sentence to death. A current of electricity will be made to pass through your bodies until you are dead. And may God have mercy on your souls. Do you have any last words?

JOEY
Joshua, Son of David, I believe. Will you remember me?

PREACHER MAN
I tell you the truth, Joey, before this day is over you and I will be together in Paradise.

JAKE
Yeah, I got a last word for you. I'll see you in hell!

> (ATTORNEY nods to RORKE who throws the switch. The condemned react, then freeze. After a moment of silence JOEY rises from his chair. There is a hatch-marked shadow on the floor, as if the light is shining through prison bars. JOEY walks into the light. Lights slowly fade on the other characters.)

JOEY
Today you will be with me in paradise. With those few words, something inside of me changed. Not the pain - for death is creeping ever closer. No, the Son of David didn't save me from this death. Rather, he gave me a new life. I was no longer a member of a family of transgressors. It was like I had a transfusion, like there was fresh, untainted blood flowing through my veins.

I've always hated Jake. He's my brother, and I've hated him.

Hated him my whole live. Now he's dying. So am I, and it's all his fault. Funny; but, for some reason, I don't hate him anymore. I don't know why. Maybe it's because, in my last moments, I've realized that being part of a family is important. In his own way, Jake was right. It's in the blood.

BLACKOUT

www.ingramcontent.com/pod-product-compliance
Lightning Source LLC
Chambersburg PA
CBHW071415290426
44108CB00014B/1831